Toby at Stony Bay

Story by Annette Smith
Illustrations by Craig Smith

"We are going to have
a busy morning, Toby,"
said B.J., as he hurried out
to his tow truck.

"What has happened?" asked Toby.

"The police have just called to say
that a boat dragged its anchor
in a storm last night.
It's been washed up on the beach
at Stony Bay," said B.J.
"We'll have to get a trailer
from the boat yard."

B.J. threw some more rope
onto the tow truck.
Then away they went down the road
to the boat yard
to pick up the trailer.

Stony Bay

The road down to Stony Bay
was very bumpy
and it made the trailer
bounce up and down.

"Slow down, Toby," called B.J.

They could see the police
waiting for them.

Toby stopped at the end of the road,
and B.J. jumped down to have a look.

"The boat has a big hole in its side,"
said the police officer,
"and it will be high tide in an hour."

The track to the sea
was blocked with huge logs
that had been tossed up
during the storm.
B.J. climbed over the logs
to have a closer look
at the boat.

"We can't get down to the boat
this way," said B.J. to Toby.
"There are huge, heavy logs
blocking the track.
What can we do?"

"They are too heavy for me to move,"
said Toby. "I can't do it!
We need a digger."

"Yes," said B.J., "you're right!
I'll get Bob to bring his digger
down here.
While we're waiting for him,
we can turn the front
of the boat around
so that it will be ready for us
to pull onto the trailer."

B.J. unhitched the trailer
and Toby backed up
as near as he could
to the boat.

"Stop here, Toby!" said B.J.
"We can't get any closer."

B.J. pulled out Toby's rope
and climbed over the rocks
and down to the boat.

Little by little, Toby turned
the front of the boat around
to face the shore.

"Good!" shouted B.J. "Now we're ready.
When Bob clears the track for us,
we can get the trailer down
to the boat."

11

Soon Bob arrived with his digger
and he set to work at once.
The digger lifted the heavy logs
out of the way,
one after the other.

"The tide is coming in,
and the wind is getting stronger again,"
called the police officer to B.J.
"Please hurry!
If the waves reach the boat,
it could break up."

"Bob has almost finished," said B.J.

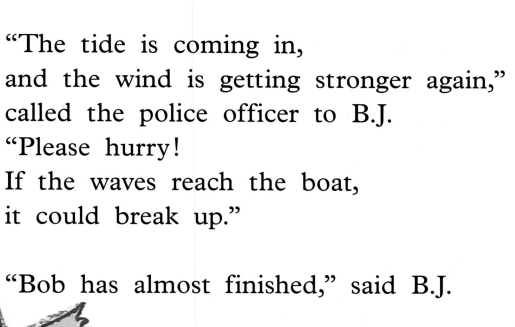

At last, Toby and B.J.
could back the trailer
down the track.
They worked as quickly
as they could,
and B.J. tied the rope
to the boat again.
By now, the waves were very close.

"Careful, Toby!" called B.J.
"We don't want the boat
to slip off the trailer.
Pull it up slowly."

When the boat was safely up
on the trailer, Toby and B.J.
were ready to leave the beach.

"Thanks for saving the boat,"
called the police officer.
"You were just in time!"

"There was nothing to it," said B.J.
"It was all in a day's work."